COMPASSION

TO

ACTION

CHRIS OVERSTREET

Compassion to Action
Copyright 2015 – Chris Overstreet

Editing: Melissa Amato
Graphic design cover: Amy Miller
Graphic design interior: Bobby Schwendenmann
Typesetting: Julie Heth
Special thanks to: Seth and Lauren Dahl

All rights reserved. This book is protected by the copyright laws of the United States of America. This book may not be copied or reprinted for commercial gain or profit. The use of short quotations or occasional page copying for personal or group study is permitted and encouraged. Permission will be granted upon request.

Unless otherwise identified, Scripture taken from the New International Version®. The Holy Bible, New International Version®, NIV® Copyright © 1973, 1978, 1984, 2011 by Biblica, Inc. TM Used by permission. All rights reserved worldwide.

Please note that the author's publishing style capitalizes certain pronouns in Scripture that refer to Father, Son, and Holy Spirit and may differ from other publishers' styles.

ISBN 13: 978-0-692-54097-8

Printed in the United States of America

DEDICATION

I want to dedicate this book to my beautiful daughter, Brielle Shalom Overstreet. Your mom and I love you so much, and we believe that God will use you to be a voice to impact this generation with the power and love of Jesus Christ working and moving through your life.

ACKNOWLEDGEMENTS

I want to thank and acknowledge Seth and Lauren Dahl for encouraging Stefanie and me to finish this book. I also want to thank Lauren for taking the time out of her busy schedule to do the first edit of this book. Thanks so much—it meant a ton.

Additionally, I would like to thank Bill Johnson, Kris Vallotton, and all the other fathers in the faith that have helped me grow in my relationship with Jesus Christ over the last 15 years. The two of you constantly inspire me to not settle, but to pursue God's best for my life.

Finally, I want to thank my wife Stefanie for championing and loving me with all your heart. Your love and support has helped me reach thousands of people for Jesus Christ.

ENDORSEMENTS

Over the past decade, I have watched Chris Overstreet grow into one of the most powerful evangelists I know. What excites me most about his life is that the zeal he carries for evangelism is ignited by love for God and people. His passion is extreme and rare—so much so that many might think they could never do what Chris does. That really is the purpose of this book. He skillfully dispels any notion that the ability to bring the love of God to people requires a certain kind of gift, or worse yet, a certain kind of personality. The love of God for people is for everyone. Discovering that love is the heart of evangelism. If you have been stuck on the bench, unsure and fearful of how to share your faith with the world around you, I encourage you to read *Compassion to Action*. It will ignite and activate something in you that will bring many to Christ and glory to God.

Bill Johnson
Senior Leader, Bethel Church, Redding, CA

Chris Overstreet's powerful new book *Compassion to Action* unearths the real meaning of the normal Christian life and teaches us how to walk in our divine mandate as evangelists and world changers. This book is a clarion call to all Believers to raise up powerful, supernatural, wonder-working Jesus people and to make disciples of all nations.

As you make your way through the pages of this book, you will find yourself on a Holy Spirit journey in which you will be inspired to walk in miracles, empowered to do the works of Jesus and equipped with the boldness to go where you have never gone before! This book is a "must read" for every Christian!

Kris Vallotton
Senior Associate Leader, Bethel Church
Redding, CA
Co-founder of the Bethel School of Supernatural Ministry
Author of eleven books, The Supernatural Ways of Royalty and Spirit Wars

---

I have known Chris for several years and was excited to have an opportunity to read and endorse his second book. He has once again given us tools and the confidence to believe God truly wants to use each of us to share His love for the lost. That is empowering! *Compassion to Action* is a book that gives encouragement to share the gospel message to those around us. It isn't difficult. It is simple when we remember the motivation behind it: God's unending love and desire for people to be set free and experience His presence. The testimonies shared in this book are truly incredible and will boost your faith and inspire you to step out and release the love of Jesus to a hurting world. You can't read this book and not be fired up and ready to step out of your comfort zones!

Chris has been working alongside Show Mercy International in Uganda, Africa for several years. He is a friend and partner in ministry. He has brought many people to serve with us and help us with our mission to the poor. Without a doubt, his teams consistently carry a love, humility and desire to serve that we seldom experience. I believe this is because of the leadership and example that Chris brings to his teams. Chris doesn't just preach or teach about evangelism and loving others, he lives it every day. It is a lifestyle, not a ministry. He believes in the people around him and desires to draw the best out of them. I love this about Chris. He has stretched me personally many times and while it can be uncomfortable, I wouldn't want it any other way. Great job on this book!

Mike Salley
Founder and Executive Director, Show Mercy International, Port Gibson, MS

It's amazing how the anointing of the evangelist is so effortlessly released through such an easily read book as Chris Overstreet's *Compassion to Action*. I personally am deeply indebted to the impact that Chris has had on my own life and ministry. As a preacher, I found it easy to minister to those inside the church, but stumbled at every turn whenever I considered those outside, the ones the Father calls us to reach out to. Chris Overstreet is not your ordinary evangelist. He's the

Ephesians 4:11-12 kind, one who can equip you to step out into an amazing partnership with the Holy Spirit that will change your world forever. You won't regret picking up this book and applying its take-home message. Your neighbourhood and city will be eternally grateful that you did.

Ian Miller
Senior Pastor of Community Church Hornsby, Sydney, Australia
National Executive Member of CRC Churches International

Over the years of observing numerous pastors and ministers, Chris has been one of the most compassionate people toward the lost and broken that I've ever known. What he writes, he lives out. He deeply loves people and burns for lost souls to know Jesus. He is a true example. In this book, you will not only receive practical keys to minister, but your heart will be set ablaze for the Gospel. You will find yourself deeper in love with Jesus as Chris shares his stories and insights. If you want a greater compassion for the lost and broken, I'd highly recommend you to read this book. Your life will never be the same!

Chris Gore
Director, Bethel Healing Rooms, Redding, CA
Author of Walking in Supernatural Healing Power

This is a great read. You will be inspired and equipped by Chris as he takes you through his personal journey (and the journey of others) of moving from fear into power and compassion. You will be convinced that no one is too old, too young, too shy, or too foolish to love other people significantly and make an eternal difference in their lives.

Steve Backlund
Global Legacy Executive Team
Co-founder of Igniting Hope Ministries
Bethel Church, Redding, CA

The Christian life is not complicated, it's simply seeing where the Father is working and joining Him. Chris Overstreet has a simple devotion that he is calling the body of Christ back too. In his book, you will get infected to love people well. Compassion to Action is not about a method to follow, but a relationship you have been brought into that God wants you to share with those around you!

Chris DeLeenheer
Partner, Rydell Holdings, Waco, TX

Chris' new book is inviting and empowering. This book will help hearts come alive again in reaching others for Christ. Whenever I meet a mighty Evangelist like Chris, I often wonder how they became so gifted, skilled and effective. In Compassion to Action, Chris points out how we all start off in the same place and with the same emotions and insecurities about sharing our faith. He then goes on to outline the steps that he personally took to grow. These steps and principles have already helped others with amazing results... I'm ready to take my next step.

Themba Malaba
Evangelist, Every Nation Churches, Southern Africa

God is preparing the saints for the greatest harvest the world has ever seen. I believe Chris Overstreet is carrying a timely message and anointing for the body of Christ to help us get ready. I have been on the streets with him and had many meals with Chris and i can say that he is as contagious and inspiring as they come! Get ready to be blessed and inspired to release what God has given you to the world!

Tom Crandall
Youth Pastor, Bethel Church, Redding CA

TABLE OF CONTENTS

INTRODUCTION	18
CHAPTER ONE: TURNING POINT	23
CHAPTER TWO: OVERCOME YOUR FEARS	33
CHAPTER THREE: EMPOWERED BY COMPASSION	41
CHAPTER FOUR: BECOME THE MESSAGE	53
CHAPTER FIVE: GOD IS ALWAYS WITH YOU	69
CHAPTER SIX: EMPOWERED BY GRACE	79
CHAPTER SEVEN: JESUS MANIFEST	95
CHAPTER EIGHT: YOU HAVE WHAT IT TAKES	105
APPENDIX ONE: MY PRAYER FOR YOU	113
APPENDIX TWO: SCRIPTURES ON COMPASSION	115
ADDITIONAL RESOURCES	125

INTRODUCTION

The cross was not about judgment, but rather a radical declaration of God's love, mercy, and compassion. Jesus was drawn to the cross out of compassion—the fuel for His life. Out of compassion Jesus fed the multitudes, healed the sick, and ultimately died on the cross.

The cross was the compassion of God in action through love and grace. It is the story of justice, deliverance from sin, and the justification that led to our redemption. His salvation purchased the ability for us to be chosen as sons and daughters. The cross makes a bold statement that without God we are rejected, but with Him and His mercy, we are accepted.

If we all got what we deserved for our sins, there would be judgment for each and every one of us. Jesus paid the price so we could receive His mercy and our judgment slate could be wiped clean. There is only One who sits on the mercy seat, and His agenda is that mercy would triumph over judgment. On Judgment Day, everyone will give an account for his or her own life. It is God's desire that none perish and all be saved. By His mercy and grace, the heavens and earth are still in existence today, and time can be extended for future sons and daughters to enter the kingdom.

His adoption agency has no prejudices against anyone. He calls all to repentance—to change the way they think and to receive the mercy of His love and grace. Everyone who receives Him is given the right to become a child of God. Their adoption papers are signed in blood, stamped, sealed, and approved by Him. He is the loving Father who wants to embrace His children into His welcoming arms.

Years ago, I had a dream of a young child standing on a box with a newspaper in his hand, saying, "Good news! Read all about it!" This young child was talking passionately about the good news of the gospel. He was excited to tell people about his Father. The child in the dream represents us, as children of God who walk in childlike faith and compassion for others. He also represents the heart of the church to tell people about the loving Father we have and how they too can know Him.

We have an opportunity to extend the mercy that was given to us by expressing a heart of compassion to others. Mercy extended is compassion in action. Every time we reach someone for Jesus, we are saying, "God, have mercy on them." When Stephen was stoned in Acts 7:59, the words that came out of his mouth were, "Lord, do not hold this sin against them." Stephen, even at his death, had mercy pouring from his blood. Jesus spilled this same mercy on the cross to deliver us from all sin and set us apart unto Him.

Mercy displayed and given to others through our lives is more powerful than judgment because it requires faith in action. If we all got what we deserved, we would be damned to hell. But God, who is rich in mercy because of His great love towards us, has adopted us into His family by His saving grace. Through grace and mercy, He has called us into relationship as children of God. As children of God, we can purpose in our hearts to abide in God's love and give to others what has been freely given to us. Let the compassion of Christ be activated through your life in order to impact the world around you. We only have one life to live, so let us live in a way that values the eternal and models the love of God.

CHAPTER ONE

TURNING POINT

"Peacemakers are the mercy of God to a sinful world."

–Heidi Baker

In 2007, I met a woman who walks in true compassion and love. Her name is Anne Evans, and for many years she walked out her compassion through simple devotion to Jesus. However, God had greater plans for Anne. He was drawing her into a life of evangelism by reaching the lost through outreach into the local community. During this season, I was spending a significant amount of time equipping and training Bethel School of Supernatural Ministry (BSSM) students how to step out in power, miraculous signs, and wonders. Anne had moved from Atlanta, Georgia, to attend the school and to pursue the things of the Spirit. She grew up knowing and loving Jesus her whole life, but the Holy Spirit was still very new to her.

Anne had always had a strong desire to be used by God, but she felt disqualified and uneducated. Being a single mom from southern Georgia and timid in personality, she disqualified herself from being used by God for powerful works. Anne had resigned herself to live a life of being content with reading the Bible and praying. However, God moved on Anne's heart and gave her a desire for greater things in and with Him. She made a radical decision to face fear and overcome her personal limitations.

While Anne was out on an outreach with me and a few others, she saw God at work in powerful ways. She thought, "That is what I want, too! I want to be used by God. I want to step out and share my faith." Anne was in her sixties before she stepped out in faith for the first time. On that outreach, a desire sparked in her heart for what is possible when a person chooses to step out with God. To this day, Anne openly professes she is not an evangelist. Instead, she has a desire to be used by God, and she allows Him to use her however He chooses. Anne has since adopted a phrase to describe how God took her from a passionless Christian walk to a life marked by walking in the strength of the Spirit. She says, "It's not time to retire—it's time to re-fire."

Jesus is faithful to use every part of our lives for His glory. As we place our lives into His hands, it removes pressure from our shoulders and empowers us to be flexible and pliable as we follow Jesus—trusting Him through the journey.

EQUIP THE SAINTS

Many years ago when I first started sharing the gospel, people who had been following Jesus longer than I had told me not everyone is an evangelist. It was presented in such a polished and loving way that I found it hard to disagree. However, there is a difference between an evangelist and those who evangelize. An evangelist is one of the five-fold gifts of Christ to help equip the church for the work of ministry. A true evangelist has a passion not just to see people saved but also to see the body of Christ equipped so they can genuinely love people as they are moved by the mercy of God. A true evangelist desires to impart the grace they have received from Jesus to the body in order to activate them in sharing the gospel. Evangelism, however, is something every believer can do.

Evangelists are equippers. Paul wrote in Ephesians 4:11-12, "Christ Himself gave the apostles, the prophets, the evangelists, the pastors and teachers to equip His people for works of service, so that the body of Christ may be built up." Meanwhile, evangelism is something every believer is called to do. "He [Jesus] said to them, 'Go into all the world and preach the gospel to all creation'" (Mark 16:15). Jesus commissioned all believers to share the gospel with all nations and all people. Matthew 28:18-20 says, "Then Jesus came to them and said, 'All authority in heaven and on earth has been given to me. Therefore, go and make disciples of all nations, baptizing them in the name of the Father and of the Son and of the Holy Spirit, and teaching them to obey everything I have commanded you. And surely I am with you always, to the very end of the age.'"

STEP OUT IN FAITH

Over the next few months, Anne consistently showed up to local outreach events in an effort to stretch herself. One day I asked Anne, "Have you ever thought about going into the nightclub with us to do ministry?"

She looked at me, shocked, and burst out, "Are you kidding me? You want me to go into the nightclub with you to do ministry?"

I was talking to a proper woman from the south with no desire to enter the young party scene. Anne felt challenged enough in her current outreach commitments. With conviction I told her, "Anne, I really feel like you need to go into the nightclub with us. You will love it. I will introduce you as Mama Anne to young people who are starving for love. All you need to do is sit down at a table, and I will invite these young clubbers to sit down next to you and allow you to pray for them. I will describe you as a God-fearing woman who hears God's voice."

Anne did not realize how great her spiritual capacity was to influence and impact others. She had spent most of her life being comfortable in church settings, but in order for her to grow, she needed to step out of her religious comfort zone that she had spent most of her life in. This is a great life lesson for all of us. Following Jesus is not always comfortable, especially if He asks us to take steps in a direction we have never been before. This will require us to activate the faith He has given us. Sometimes, just like Gideon (see Judges chapters 6-7), we have to go even when we are afraid, trusting God is with us every step of the way.

After our discussion, Anne went and sought the Lord in prayer about what I was asking of her. She came back a week later and said, "Well, Chris, I prayed about it. And although I'm afraid, I feel like I'm supposed to do this."

I assured her, "Anne, you will love it! This is going to be great!"

That same week, Anne started going to nightclubs with me. The young people we met there were drawn to her, attracted by the light and hope she carried. Anne would prophesy and pray over anyone who sat with her. Many of the young people were radically impacted by the wisdom, truth, and joy she spoke into their lives. I saw Anne come alive in this environment. For about a year after that first night in the club, she would gather teams and go into the clubs on her own. Under her leadership, the ministry came alive and many people were set free from a life of sin. It wasn't long before I made the decision to turn the ministry over to Anne, and it continued to thrive as her heart of compassion grew into action.

One night at the nightclub, the music was pounding, and Anne had an idea to create a dance tunnel similar to the one on the TV show Soul Train. People would walk through the tunnel thinking it was just there for dancing, while the team would lay hands on the people and pray for them. The first people to go through the tunnel were Anne's ministry team. As they walked through and began laughing, dancing, and enjoying the goodness of God, other individuals from the dance floor began to come over. What the clubbers did not realize is they were being set up for an encounter with God. The music was so loud they could not hear the team praying for them. These people were feeling the effects of prayer as supernatural joy filled their bodies.

After going through the tunnel, a young lady turned to one of Anne's team leaders, Candace, and asked her, "What are you drinking tonight?"

Candace responded, "I'm not drinking anything."

The young lady asked, "So, what are you on?"

Candace answered, "I'm not using anything. I'm a Christian. I am happy like this all the time."

She said, "You're a Christian? What are you doing here?"

Candace replied, "We are here because of you guys. Jesus loves you." Candace proceeded to pray for her and watched as the effects of God's love began to overcome the temporary buzz of alcohol in this young woman's life.

SOULS SAVED IN THE NIGHTCLUB

As Anne consistently showed up at the nightclub, the bouncers began to share with her that the atmosphere was significantly calmer with the presence of the team there, compared to when they were not there. It was becoming increasingly evident that Anne's team was having a positive influence on the party scene in Redding.

On another night, Anne and her team member, Jimmy Jack, were playing pool with some individuals from the nightclub. They started a conversation with a young man, Justin, who was a regular at the nightclub. He was searching to fill the empty void consuming his heart.

As they were talking, Justin asked, "What kind of church do you go to?"

Justin was extremely intoxicated that night, but when Anne and Jimmy began to share the gospel in the midst of his intoxication, the Word of God was taking root in his heart. Jesus was standing before Justin, and He was knocking on his heart.

Anne did not really have the words to describe the church she went to in a short amount of time. Suddenly, in that nightclub where MTV and raunchy music videos are the norm, God TV came on one of the televisions. Misty Edwards was worshipping the Lord on the big screen positioned right beside the pool table. Anne pointed to the TV screen and said, "Well, we kind of go to a church like that. It's called Bethel Church."

After having the gospel presented to him, Justin gave his life to Jesus Christ. He was then baptized. Not much later, Justin found out about the Bethel School of Supernatural Ministry. He went on to attend the school, and his whole life has been forever changed.

I think about the lives that were changed in that nightclub, and it leads me to wonder what would have happened if Anne Evans never overcame her fear of stepping into that nightclub? What is possible in your life if you make the choice to overcome your fear? Seven years later, Anne Evans is still stepping out to minister to people daily while helping to activate others to do the same. If you were to ask Anne if she would consider herself an evangelist, she would respond with a blatant "No." Anne has simply made a decision to be an obedient witness of Jesus Christ, operating in love and compassion and allowing this to move her heart into action.

YOU CAN DO IT

As you are reading this book, I want you to feel empowered. I want you to feel encouraged. I want you to feel like you also can be a witness for Jesus Christ. The wonderful thing about Jesus is He does not just extend all His grace through one personality type and say, "These ones are going to see souls saved." Instead, He pours His grace and His Spirit out on the body of Christ so we all can impact the world.

If you are a doctor, a lawyer, a teacher, or have another profession, you may never stand behind a pulpit inside the church. However, God has anointed you and has provided you with a pulpit of your own. It is important each of us realize the influence we currently have and the daily opportunities God provides to impact people with His love and power. Our lives are constantly speaking and sending out messages to the people who are close to us, many times without us even talking. Frequently in the work place, our lives lived out become the pulpit and the sermon. The truth is, the best sermons in the world are often not what is preached, but what is consistently lived out by ordinary people who love God and others around them.

My desire is to help you recognize your pulpit and platform. This will help you discover how you can put compassion into action and help you see people become saved through the power of the Holy Spirit moving in your life.

Anne Evans is an ordinary person just like you. She did not consider herself an evangelist. She is naturally quiet and reserved, but she trusted a feeling inside of her heart that said, "I think there is more to this Christian life than just going to church." She trusted the Holy Spirit would move through her to see souls saved.

> *Hello! I just want to encourage every believer to overcome your fears, and to step into all God has created you to be! If I had never faced my fears, which were keeping me from walking out the dream I had in my heart to do, I never would have known how much God wanted to and was willing to use me supernaturally to demonstrate his love and power to a hopeless and hungry world. Every obstacle is just an opportunity to overcome and be the powerful person you were created to be! Jesus can't wait to partner with each of you and amaze you at what He will do through you!*
>
> *—Mama Anne*

How can I practically apply this in my life?

___

What are the action steps I can take today to help incorporate this in my life?

___

CHAPTER TWO

OVERCOME YOUR FEARS

"He is no fool who gives what he cannot keep to gain what he cannot lose."

-Jim Elliot

While in South Africa years ago, I was given an amazing invitation to stay at a mountain retreat center. One night around the barbecue, the owners told us they would like to give us an opportunity to rappel down a mountainside. I was co-leading this trip, and to my surprise, everyone was excited about this opportunity except for me. Fear was running through my mind as I contemplated this opportunity. My mind was fixated on thoughts of the rope snapping and the potential of dying as I attempted to rappel down the mountain. Fear fed me thousands of reasons why I could not do this.

The owner was adamant that we would be rappelling before we left, and honestly, I was hoping he would forget. When the day came, everyone was still excited except for me. I attempted to muster up any excuse as to why I could not participate. The owner of the lodge began to get angry with me. He was frustrated that I was leading the team, but I was not willing to take a risk myself.

I watched as my whole team rappelled down the mountain. Although the mountain was only about 150 to 200 feet, I refused to put my harness on. He told me repeatedly, "Put your harness on and rappel down the mountain."

I firmly said, "No, I can't."

Finally, in frustration, he saw fear was trying to control me. He looked me right in the eye and said, "You're going down that mountain."

Fear spoke back at him as I replied, "No, I'm not."

"Yes, you are."

Then the Lord began to speak to me, reminding me of the words spoken in 2 Timothy 1:7, "For the Spirit God gave us does not make us timid, but gives us power, love and self-discipline."

The owner of the retreat center took my harness and began to treat me like a child. He put that harness on me and said, "You are going down this mountain."

After much disagreement, I finally gave up. "Fine," I said. "I will do it. What do I need to do?"

He gave me some simple instructions. I had never been

so afraid in my life. My heart felt as if it could have beaten right out of my chest. As I slowly began to descend the mountain's edge, my anxiety began to lift. Crawling my way down the mountain, about 50 feet away from the ground, I realized, "Wow, this is not too bad. I actually enjoy this. I can do this!" God used that instructor to help me overcome fear. Is there anyone in your life who will challenge you to do the same?

Fear attempted to hold me back from discovering a new activity I really enjoyed, but I needed someone to push me over the edge. A sound mind empowers you to make decisions out of the will of God—doing what He says you can do and making the impossible possible. I needed a literal boost out of fear and into freedom. Although it began with a struggle, I enjoyed rappelling so much that I went back up the mountain and came down one more time on my own. No matter the circumstance, I want you to feel like you can overcome your fear too. All it takes is a little encouragement—and sometimes a push in the right direction.

If evangelism and sharing your faith is like jumping off a mountaintop to you, I have good news for you: You are not alone. God's Holy Spirit will hold you up and help you the whole time. Every day we have the chance to make numerous choices. Together, let's make the choice to ask the Holy Spirit to help us demonstrate compassion with action as a lifestyle.

Jesus invites each of us on a journey of compassion, and compassion is often activated through faith. Sometimes we might not feel the emotion of compassion, but that should never prevent us from believing the most compassionate One lives inside of us and wants to love through us. Regardless of your personality or your gifting, if your desire is to be used by God, He will use you.

LOVE OVERCOMES FEAR

Sometimes when I get up to speak to a large crowd, or even a small crowd, I can suddenly get nervous. When this happens, I scan the room of people I am afraid of speaking to, and say silently to myself, "I love you, I love you, I love you" as I look into their eyes. The more I focus on love, the less I feel fear. 1 John 4:18 says, "There is no fear in love. But perfect love drives out fear, because fear has to do with punishment." Fear involves torment, but love brings peace of mind. When you make the choice to consistently choose to love people, you don't have time to fear them.

The disciples had just returned from a short-term mission trip, and they told Jesus all the things they had done and taught. Afterwards they were traveling by boat to a quiet place for some rest, but many people saw them, recognized them, and went to the place the boat landed. Mark 6:34 explains, "And Jesus, when He came out, saw a great multitude and was moved with compassion for them, because they where like sheep not having a shepherd. So He began to teach them many things." Compassion moved Jesus to see the multitude like sheep that needed a shepherd, and compassion activated Him to teach them. After teaching, He not only wanted to provide for them spiritually, but also physically.

I imagine the disciples were tired and frustrated by the time they asked Jesus to send the multitudes away. They had just returned from mission trips and then had been with the crowd all day. They wanted some rest and something to eat. Jesus, however, had another plan. He wanted to feed the entire crowd. The disciples only saw five loaves and two fish as their resources. Jesus saw food from heaven, His compassion pulled it down, and He asked the disciples to feed the multitudes with it. The disciples could have let fear stop them from giving away the little food they had, but they chose to partner with Jesus instead. They fed 5,000 people that evening, not by focusing on what they did not have, but by presenting what little they did have in the hands of Jesus. With Jesus there is always enough.

Don't wait for the feeling of faith—just go for it. Sometimes you just need to step out in faith, even though you're feeling afraid. I thank God that He can use people like you and me that have dealt with fear. You need to know you are not alone. Many people in the Bible dealt with fear, such as Abraham, Moses, Jacob, Gideon, Saul, Peter, Paul, Timothy…the list goes on and on. Just because we feel fear does not mean we have to bow down to it. Trust in God and keep moving forward in faith, knowing that love overcomes fear.

WHAT IS IN YOUR HANDS?

You might not feel like you have much to give, but if you put what you do have in the hands of Jesus, it will be multiplied. Don't wait to feel compassionate to be compassionate. Make the choice to live a compassionate life, trusting that the most compassionate One who ever walked on earth lives inside you. There have been times when God has asked me to do something I did not feel capable of, nor did I feel the emotion of compassion. But when I stepped out, the compassionate One who lives within me came out to touch the one who was in need.

Each person has been given something to contribute to society for the better of others, so don't let fear hold you back. Don't be the person that hides your talent in the ground, hoping to play it safe in life. The safest place to be is in the perfect will of God, while loving every person who God places in your life.

How can I practically apply this in my life?

What are the action steps I can take today to help incorporate this in my life?

CHAPTER THREE

EMPOWERED BY COMPASSION

"Great faith doesn't come out of great effort, but out of great surrender."

—Bill Johnson

In 2007, my wife and I went to visit her parents in Portland for the holidays. A week before Christmas Day, I decided to ride the train downtown for some last minute gift shopping. As I stepped off the train, I saw a young girl around 17 or 18 years old. She was sitting on a curb with her head between her legs. My heart automatically went out to her, and I could feel something was not right.

I went over to her and tapped her on her shoulder. "Excuse me, are you okay?" I asked. She was reluctant to respond. I continued, "My name is Chris. What's your name?"

With a dazed look, she responded, "My name is Grace."

As she looked up, I could tell she was not in a good place. She told me she was withdrawing from heroin and had not slept in a while. I asked her if she was hungry. I noticed a fast food place about 100 yards away and asked her if I could buy her a sandwich. She said that would be nice because she was very hungry.

As we went to the restaurant, Grace could only walk about 15 feet before stopping and nearly passing out. This lasted for only a few minutes, but it felt as if traveling the short distance took hours. We finally arrived at the restaurant, and she ordered some food. As we waited for the food to be ready, I asked Grace some questions to get to know her a little.

She said she had been on the streets for a while. During our conversation, something happened that I would never forget. As I looked into this young lady's eyes, I saw Jesus looking directly back at me. His gaze pierced me, and it felt like He looked right into my heart. In that moment, it was as if He was talking to me. Without words being said, I could feel His heart. I could hear Him ask, "How will you treat Me in this moment?" I was shocked because nothing like this had ever happened to me before, and I have ministered to many people. I was looking into the face of Jesus through a young girl's face.

Then I noticed a gentleman across from us, eating a sandwich. I said, "Grace, stay here for a minute. Just trust me."

I said to the gentleman, "This is Grace. She is like my sister, and she's just coming off heroin. I have to go take care of something quickly. Will you watch her for just five minutes and make sure she doesn't leave?"

I walked around the area, searching for a hotel. Suddenly I came across a very nice hotel. The Lord asked me to help her by putting her up in the hotel. I walked up to the reception desk and said, "I need your help. My sister Grace is in a really bad condition right now. She is just coming off heroin, and she needs to sleep here for the night. May I please rent a room for her?" The receptionist agreed. All I could manage to say was "Thank you" as I walked away in excitement.

I went back to the fast food restaurant and said, "Grace, somebody has helped you. Someone paid for you to stay at a nice hotel."

She looked at me in shock and wonder and asked, "Who did this?"

As I brought Grace to the front desk, I asked the bellman if he would accompany us to the room to show Grace where she would be staying. I asked him to show her all the room had to offer. As I left with the bellman, I told Grace how much God loved her and assured her He had a plan for her life. That night I had seen Jesus face to face through Grace's face.

Two days later, I was in the city again. I looked to see if Grace was around. I wanted to check on her and see how she was doing. I asked a couple of young guys that were around the first day I had seen her. One of them asked, "Are you talking about Grace? The prostitute?"

I was shocked. "What do you mean? Is she a prostitute?"

They said, "Oh yeah, she's a prostitute."

I realized the other night, Grace had likely experienced God's pure love for the very first time.

MATTHEW 25:31-40

When the Son of Man comes in His glory, and all the angels with Him, He will sit on His glorious throne. All the nations will be gathered before Him, and He will separate the people one from another as a shepherd separates the sheep from the goats. He will put the sheep on His right and the goats on His left.

Then the King will say to those on His right, "Come, you who are blessed by My Father; take your inheritance, the kingdom prepared for you since the creation of the world. For I was hungry and you gave Me something to eat, I was thirsty and you gave Me something to drink, I was a stranger and you invited Me in, I needed clothes and you clothed Me, I was sick and you looked after Me, I was in prison and you came to visit Me."

Then the righteous will answer Him, "Lord, when did we see You hungry and feed You, or thirsty and give You something to drink? When did we see You a stranger and invite You in, or needing clothes and clothe You? When did we see You sick or in prison and go to visit You?"

The King will reply, "Truly I tell you, whatever you did for one of the least of these brothers and sisters of Mine, you did for Me."

That day God taught me something about Himself. He is hidden in those who we often pass by. I will never forget the look He gave me while I looked into Grace's eyes. It was the look of a caring Father, hoping His daughter would be looked after with love.

Over the years, I have heard many philosophies centered on helping the poor. Some lean towards not helping them at all so they will "wake up and smell the coffee." When I look at the life of Jesus, I see a great example of love poured out for us. Love is the ultimate way to help those in need.

POWER IS IN LOVE

God's love is so powerful. We all were like Grace at one time—lost, cold, and dying inside. That is why God sent His Son to help us, to restore us, and to bring life into our hearts. Every one of us had Jesus come and take us out of darkness and into His marvelous light. Jesus looks at us and knows we are worth it. God's love is the strongest force in the universe. It empowers us to see from His perspective. With our natural eyes, we cannot see very clearly. But with the eyes of God's love, we are able to spot the value He sees in people. Colossians 3:14 says, "And over all these virtues put on love, which binds them all together in perfect unity." The most powerful motivator is God's love.

I often have people approach me who want to be activated in the gifts of the Spirit. I love their enthusiasm and passion. However, my heart is not just to see someone activated in spiritual gifts. I want to see people activated in the love that empowers these gifts to naturally flow through their lives. When you choose to love someone, it takes the pressure to perform off of you, and everything begins to flow from your heart. The gifts of the Holy Spirit are most powerful and effective when demonstrated through love.

The world we live in needs the power of God and, at the same time, the power of God's love. God's love and power are never supposed to be separated because God's love truly is the power of God. God's love sent Jesus to die in our place and take on our sin so we could be in right standing with Him. It was God's love on display that created the largest adoption movement, adopting sons and daughters from every tribe, tongue, and nation into His eternal Kingdom. We discover in God's love that He desires none to perish.

THE MINISTRY OF THE BELIEVER

Every believer has been given at least three ministries. The first one is to love and worship God as a lifestyle. The second ministry is to love one another and to be in right relationship with each other as believers. Our third ministry is to share our faith and demonstrate compassion to those who are in need. It is this third ministry we will no longer be able to do once we get into heaven. We will be able to be in 24/7 worship and adoration to the King of Kings. We also will have all of eternity for fellowship with other believers, but we will not have the opportunity to participate in sharing our faith and demonstrating compassion to those in need. This ministry was created for us only while we are on the earth.

God's desire is for a healthy, loving family. He does not want people to be separated and living outside of family. He is the author of family; He created each of us to be in a family. God has a big dinner table, and He loves to celebrate with family. Even before the foundation of the world, He has been planning the largest party in all of history. This party will include His extended family from every nation, tribe, and tongue.

God's love and power are so strong that they can move through any denomination and any person who professes to be a believer in Jesus Christ. They can move through any believer who has a personal relationship with Jesus. Love is what compelled God to send His only Son to save the world. "For God so loved the world that He gave His one and only Son, that whoever believes in Him shall not perish but have eternal life" (John 3:16). Once we experience what is possible in our own lives by the saving grace of God, it is the love He expresses through us that compels us to share Him with others. "For Christ's love compels us, because we are convinced that one died for all, and therefore all died" (2 Corinthians 5:14).

Throughout the years I have had the honor to travel and preach in many different countries. I have sat in many homes, some small and some large, where I have had the privilege to observe families and their cultures. It always amazes and excites me when I hear testimonies of God working through ordinary people in powerful ways in different cultures and settings. As I listen closely to the stories of the miracles God is doing, I wish people who say God is not moving in power any more could hear these testimonies.

When we are submitted to the purposes of God, all dividing forces crumble in our midst. We see God is not a respecter of persons, nor is He a respecter of a certain culture or denomination. God wants to move through every denomination and culture that has a desire for Him to move in and through them. Denominations are often a reflection of a belief system about who they feel God is and what God wants to do through them. God is bigger than our differences, and His love has the power to open wide the hearts of all believers to be able to say, "I can be used by God in extraordinary ways too." When we look throughout history, we see God moving in raw power throughout different denominations, and it is wonderful to see the expression of Jesus Christ manifest within them.

If you are a part of a denomination or church right now where you are not experiencing what you desire, do not lose hope. Do not give up. God wants to pour out on you. He wants to pour His Spirit out on all flesh—not just a particular denomination or church or type of person. The Word of God never highlights one denomination or culture, but instead it highlights believers.

John 14:12 says, "Very truly I tell you, whoever believes in Me will do the works I have been doing, and they will do even greater things than these, because I am going to the Father." It is God's perfect will that believers, regardless of denomination, would move in signs and wonders and do the greater works Jesus promised.
I have discovered that God loves surprising us. The Spirit of God is attracted to us if we have a hungry heart and a humble attitude that says, "God, my life is significant

because You created me. I believe You can use me." We are empowered by God's grace to be used by Him in extraordinary ways. I believe the Lord is breaking down spiritual pride in our churches so He may use His church collectively to be an expression of His hands and feet throughout all the earth. He wants to use believers who are united by their love for Christ rather than divided in pride. Spiritual pride says, "I know it all. I have the full revelation of Jesus, and there is nothing for me to learn from anyone else." If we remain humble and teachable, we will be surprised by what we can learn from each other.

KEEP YOUR EYES ON JESUS

The devil lies and tells people within the church that God only moves in certain ways through specific denominations. He tries to get people to focus on denominational differences and have them create more of an emotional connection to their denomination and its belief system than to Jesus Himself. Jesus wants to partner with us all, regardless of our denomination or background. The truth is that God wants nothing to hold you back from your destiny and from shaping the course of eternity.

The world's greatest need right now is to experience the tangible love of God expressed through relationship with Jesus Christ. God wants to use every denomination in the expansion of His kingdom coming to earth. The wonderful thing about Jesus is not only did He pay for every tribe and tongue to be saved, but He also paid for every denomination to have an understanding that we are all on the same winning team. As a team, many of us have different functions, but we are all focused on one goal: to win. Together as a team, our common vision is to win souls to Christ and see His kingdom expanded on earth. God is not leaving you on the bench. It is time to run on the field and put into play all you have been practicing in past seasons so we can see Jesus get the great victory!

How can I practically apply this in my life?

What are the action steps I can take today to help incorporate this in my life?

CHAPTER FOUR

BECOME THE MESSAGE

"God has given us two hands, one to receive with the and the other to give with."

–Billy Graham

Years ago, I had the privilege of meeting with a BSSM student named Jason Chin. As Jason and I sat down together, he expressed he had many fears about stepping out to share the gospel. He had received a lot of great teaching at school, but something was still holding him back from sharing his faith.

Bethel School of Supernatural Ministry is designed to activate the students in what they are learning. This way what they learn does not remain just a theory, but there is practical application outside the four walls of the church. Jason had previously skipped some of his assigned school outreaches due to fear.

After talking with me and a few others, Jason decided he

would no longer let fear control him. That summer, after he had graduated from BSSM, he made a decision that he would share the gospel with at least one person every day. Although it was scary, he was committed to growth. The more he stepped out and shared his faith, the more relaxed he became. Jason found his strength in love. He found the more he focused on loving people, the less powerful fear became. Fear lost its grip every time Jason began to focus on love. When you and I focus on God's love, fear loses its hold and manipulating power. God's love is what helps activate us into a lifestyle of compassion.

Whether we realize it or not, we are often witnessing. We share with others about how our day is going or about the weather. Sometimes people will talk ten minutes with a stranger about the weather. It is interesting how we can feel comfortable talking to a stranger about the weather, but we are afraid to share the gospel with them. We feel afraid to address an issue bigger than the weather—the condition of their heart. God wants to encourage us that if we can talk about the weather, we can take it a little bit further and talk about how He loves them and wants to change the condition of their heart.

DESTROY THE WORKS OF THE DEVIL

If a family had a child trapped in a burning house, the parents' priority would be saving the child. The father would have urgency in his heart to do whatever he could to rescue his child. The number one thing that child would need is to be rescued from the fire—to be saved. Likewise, we need to have urgency in our hearts for God's children to be saved. I am not downplaying interacting with others and talking about the weather, nor do I think it is wise to treat everyone like a project with a goal of them praying a prayer of salvation. What I am trying to communicate is that we must value and have compassion for the condition of the human soul.

Every person is important to God, and every person has spiritual needs. This is why it is vital to be aware of the condition of the heart and spiritual needs each person has. I believe God gives us wisdom to discern where people are at on their journey towards faith in Him. Sometimes He will use us to plant a seed, and other times God will use us to reap the harvest. We have to be okay with the both of them. If we feel confident to comment to somebody on the weather, then God can give us the confidence to bring up the subject of His love and saving grace that is available for everyone who trusts in Him.

ACTIVATE WHAT YOU'VE BEEN GIVEN

Have you ever been to a conference where the speaker gave an altar call? Imagine being at a conference and listening to your favorite speaker. At the end, there is an altar call about being used more by God. You respond. With great emotion, you say, "God, do whatever You want to do with my life. I will do anything for You."

That night you go to bed and you pray again, "God use me."

The next morning, God starts talking to you. He says something like, "Talk to your neighbor about Me."

You pause and say, "God, is that You?"

He whispers in your heart one more time, "Talk to your neighbor about Me."

You pray for another confirmation, "Reveal to me, Lord, whether or not this is really You. Do You really want me to tell my neighbor You love them?"

Then you ask in prayer as you go through your day, "God, do You really want me to talk to my neighbor?"

You find yourself having a very busy day. You go to bed that night and pray, "Lord, please use me. I want to be used by You."

The next morning God speaks to you as you are getting ready for work, "Tell your neighbor I love them and have a plan for their life."

You pause, and again ask, "God, is this really You?"

This happens all the time. We ask God to use us and to empower us to arise so we can shine, and then He begins to talk to us. He whispers in our heart, whether it is in the grocery store or at work, and in that moment, we have a choice to make. We can choose to arise and answer the call of God on our life or not. When we have a "yes" in our heart, God will shine through us.

I can imagine someone finally responding to God's voice telling them to speak to their neighbor. Maybe months have gone by before they give in to the voice of the Lord and say, "Okay God, I will finally speak to my neighbor."

They prepare a gift and make their way over to their neighbor's house. Secretly, they say in their heart, "If they don't come to the door after I knock a couple of times, I will leave."

As they knock on the door, they wait for a moment. No one comes to the door. They decide to knock one more time. If no one comes, they are planning on making a quick exit. After ringing the doorbell a second time, someone comes to the door. They introduce themselves, and they finally say, "Hello, my name is... I am your neighbor. This might sound very strange to you, but I have been praying that God would speak to me and use me. He keeps on bringing you to my mind. He wants me to tell you He loves you and has a plan for your life."

Unexpectedly, the neighbor responds with enthusiasm. But, at the same time, he is embarrassed. He says, "Wow, thanks so much for coming over here and telling me this. I have lived at this house for the last 15 years. When you moved in a couple years ago, the Lord put it in my heart to tell you Jesus loves you as well and has a plan for your life. I think you beat me to it."

Sometimes God is calling us out of our boats in order to empower us to overcome fear as we walk on water to meet Him. Isn't it funny we can live such busy lives that we do not know who our neighbors are? Maybe God wants to bring neighbors together to pray together and to see their neighborhood transformed for the glory of God. Often we hear testimonies of God touching areas stricken by poverty, but what about middle class or wealthy neighborhoods? These people need Jesus just as much as the poor. Without Jesus, we all are poor and in need of a Savior.

When we discover God has already awakened our hearts, it creates awareness inside of us that we have something to offer which is so valuable and precious. It has the power to shift eternity. When we say "Yes" to Jesus, He will make a way to communicate His love and power through our lives. I have realized in my own life that every day is a choice. Today, I believe God is empowering you to say, "Yes, I will choose to put my compassion into action."

The first step you must take in being activated to step out in compassion is realizing you already have a heart of compassion and your life is a witness to others. The way you live your life speaks louder than your words, but God wants to use your words as well. Our mouth is such a powerful tool. When we speak with love, it has the ability to change environments around us and soften others' hearts as we partner with the Holy Spirit.

You are a testimony, and you have been bought by the blood of Jesus Christ. Knowing and believing this truth disarms the performance mentality that tries to have you reach the lost for the sake of "getting testimonies." Your life is the testimony. This revelation will mobilize you to love people through experiencing first hand the power that is in God's saving grace.

JESUS AT YOUR WORK PLACE

Throughout life, we interact with many types of people: family, coworkers, friends, and strangers. Every day we can ask God for eyes of love—eyes to see people the way God sees them. Love takes the pressure off us and provides a platform to share the gospel with others. When the people around us consistently experience God's love through our lives, they will see that the words we say and the life we live are consistent. This builds trust in their hearts. As God provides an opportunity for us to share the gospel, their hearts are then more open to receive God's truth. Our lives speak louder than our words.

If an employee talks about Jesus at work and shares what Jesus has done to transform their life, but he or she is a terrible employee, then their witness will often times be ineffective. But if someone is a great employee and shares about Jesus and the transformation they've had, it can be very effective. Jesus is with us at work, and we get the privilege of releasing His presence while we steward our jobs well. When we work with excellence and a positive attitude, our lives become an invitation to others.

It is extremely important to keep the gospel simple. The gospel of the Kingdom was never meant to be an intellectual debate, nor was it designed to entertain minds. The gospel penetrates hearts. The Bible says the testimony of Jesus Christ is the spirit of prophecy (Revelation 19:10). When you share with others what Jesus Christ has done for you, it creates faith in the atmosphere for others to believe their lives can also be changed.

Sharing about the Kingdom of God is meant to be fun, and we can learn to have fun when sharing the simple but powerful gospel. It is the expression of life coming out of us. There is a weight to the truth of the gospel, but it is meant to be shared through love and joy, not heaviness. The goodness of God is what leads people to repentance. We can become a walking invitation to the good news of Jesus Christ by living a life marked by integrity, releasing His joy and compassion, and loving the people in our lives.

THE JOY OF SALVATION

Many years ago when I first started sharing my faith, I found I would be so serious and intense that I lacked joy; I did not see the fun in saving souls. My attitude was negatively affecting how people perceived me on the streets and negatively affecting the way I would share the gospel. Many times when people step out and share their faith, they become burnt out when it is not done in fun. They make it a serious and hard job, instead of letting it be a life-giving expression of God's love and power. Do not be too serious, but rather learn to have fun. No one wants to become a depressed Christian. There is so much joy in experiencing God's salvation, and you get to express this joy. Jesus is the ultimate expression of joy to the world.

While there is urgency in the gospel, God does not want us to be depressed messengers, but Spirit-filled bringers of joy instead. "Nehemiah said, 'Go and enjoy choice food and sweet drinks, and send some to those who have nothing prepared. This day is holy to our Lord. Do not grieve, for the joy of the Lord is your strength'" (Nehemiah 8:10). God's joy gives us strength. Joy is a fruit of the Spirit (Galatians 5:22), and spending time with God will grow your joy.

You may find yourself in a situation where you do not know what to say. We have all been there before, and that is why the Helper, the Holy Spirit, is there to give us the right words in each situation. He will flow through us. We can trust Him with all of our hearts, knowing He wants people to get saved more than we do. The Holy Spirit loves pointing people to Jesus. He is the best evangelist. Trust that the Spirit is leading in your life and learn to be sensitive to His voice. I have found the best way to develop sensitivity to the voice of God is by praying when no one else is around, asking God questions, and listening for His direction and His voice. This is essential. When you know God's voice, you will be able to respond in situations when you do not know what to say. He will give you the words to say.

Like many of you, I live in an environment where there are many gifted people. When you are around gifted people, there is a tendency and a challenge to want to be like them. Maybe you even feel intimidated by their strengths. I have found being comfortable in your own skin is so powerful. I truly do not desire to be like anyone else.

Years ago, when I first came on staff at Bethel Church as the Outreach Pastor, I struggled. I compared my gifts to other leaders around me. Through times of prayer and God speaking to me, He revealed to me that I am the best Chris Overstreet when I am not focusing on trying to be like someone else. It was so simple, but so powerful. God is not looking to make clones. God has placed something unique in your life.

Your personality is amazing. He designed you in such a way that no one else can be like you. We can learn from people and need others around us, but we become our best and most effective when we become confident in God's love for us as the individuals He made us to be. When we discover God loves us so deeply and He is the one who designed us and wired us, we realize God can use us supernaturally and powerfully. His use of us, however, might not look like His use of anybody else.

One of the best ways to create a lifestyle of sharing your faith is to ask God for His heart for people. Then begin to imagine loving the people He loves and interacting with them in the way He reveals to you. My goal for you is not that you would look like anyone else or you impersonate someone else's style, but you would discover how God wants you to share your faith with others around you. My wife is a wonderful example of this. Stefanie is quiet by nature. She is not loud like me, but she has a "yes" inside her heart. There are times when we are out and about in the community, and the way she approaches and talks to people is completely different from the way I do.

One particular example happened after an evangelism training meeting I did in Michigan. Stefanie and I, along with one other friend, went to Subway after the session. We went up to order our food, and Stefanie asked the gentleman who was helping us how his day was. He said, "It's my birthday."

She said, "Really? You want to know what we do for people when it's their birthday?"

I had no idea what she was going to say because I had no idea what the answer was. We didn't have a set way of celebrating people's birthdays.

He asked hesitantly, "What do you do?"

She said, "We give them encouraging words. Can we give you an encouraging word?"

He responded in a curious tone, "Yes."

We proceeded to encourage him and prophesy over him. Jesus Christ radically impacted that man's life and birthday. I think it is very important that you discover your style of approach. In order for you to discover your style of approach, it is very important for you to begin to take steps. At first, stepping out might feel very uncomfortable, especially if you have never talked to a stranger before about Jesus. It might not be your norm, but the good news is after you do it for a while, you realize the Holy Spirit lives inside of you, and He is the greatest evangelist. He will always help you.

I bought a bike years ago because I was training for a half-Ironman triathlon. I never knew how to clip in and out of the special pedals. No one ever really taught me. However, I was excited to learn. I rode my bike out of the bike shop and within a hundred yards, there was a four way stop intersection. I was having a blast riding my new bike, but I also had a big problem—I could not click my foot out to stop my bike. I was either going to run directly into traffic and weave through all the cars, or I would have to make the decision to slow down as much as I could and make myself fall over because my feet would not come out of the clips on the pedals. I chose the second option. As I lie on the ground, the people in the cars at the stoplight looked over at me. I imagine they thought, "He must've just bought that bike. He is a rookie."

In that moment, I had a choice: Do I get back up and continue to ride my bike, or do I say to myself, "Biking is not for me?" I chose to get back up and ride my bike.

Although the first couple of months were difficult for me to get used to the pedals, now it has become easy. I don't even think twice about pedaling—it comes naturally to me now. Clipping in and clipping out has become a natural part of cycling in my life. The truth that you "can do all things through Christ" (Philippians 4:13) is going to become more natural the more you step out.

Sometimes when we step out in faith, we do not feel comfortable. It is not our normal. It's just like riding my new bike was not my normal, but the passion to finish a triathlon gave me the persistence to keep going forward. Your passion and love for Jesus will give you persistence so you do not quit, but instead say, "I realize I will make mistakes on the journey, but the Holy Spirit is helping me."

A NOTE FROM MY WIFE, STEFANIE

I gave my life to Christ at a young age and had a wonderful experience attending church as I grew up.

The only type of evangelism I had been exposed to was method-based. To me, it felt like trying to convince someone about why they should follow Jesus. I'm not a naturally persuasive person, so this method never felt like it fit me. I decided to leave evangelism up to other believers because I thought it wasn't my gift.

In my early 20s, I received a prophetic word about evangelism being birthed in my heart and being a part of reaching millions of people for the Lord. That word didn't fit the current state of my life—at that time, I didn't want much to do with evangelism because I was afraid of it! But I thought about that word during the following weeks, and I realized it was an invitation. I felt like I could see fruit in the area of evangelism by partnering with that word, or I could ignore it. In this instance, I really felt that in order for that word to come to pass, I would have to choose to partner with it.

Shortly after, I moved to Redding, CA and joined Bethel Church. I became involved in the outreach ministries because I knew I would have opportunities to overcome my fears about evangelism and partner with the word I had received. During this process, I learned from Chris and others that evangelism is actually really simple. It's about loving people and sharing God's love and the message of Jesus with them. I didn't need to convince people of anything because I learned just how powerful a demonstration of God's love really can be. And I also learned that evangelism is more than a gift—it's a calling for all believers.

I realized that since I'm called to evangelism as a follower of Jesus, He desires to use my unique personality and gifts to share His love with others. I've found that God loves to use the fact that I'm naturally an encourager to reach people with His love. For me, it's as simple as partnering with the Holy Spirit to give someone an encouraging word and share His love with them. I overcame my fears by gradually taking risks and encouraging others. The knowledge of how much God loves me and wants to use me to share His love with others was what helped me overcome my fears.

My heart's desire is that you would discover your calling to evangelism as a follower of Jesus. Not only that, but I want to encourage you to discover how God has uniquely designed you to reach others with His love. This journey has truly been rewarding, and partnering with God to share His love brings great joy. My hope is that you would experience this for yourself.

How can I practically apply this in my life?

What are the action steps I can take today to help incorporate this in my life?

CHAPTER FIVE

GOD IS ALWAYS WITH YOU

"Some unanswered prayers are only because God doesn't want to do something for us. He wants to do something through us."

–Bill Johnson

The Holy Spirit lives in every believer—He never leaves you alone. Many times we might not feel anything, but we need to trust God is with us. There is a difference between moving in power and moving in authority. Power is when you feel God is resting on you. You feel anything is possible. You know something is about to happen because you can feel it. It is like riding a wave; you feel the momentum of the Spirit.

Authority is a little different. When moving in authority, you do not necessarily feel anything, but you know God has called you. You know God is with you. God has given authority to every believer. When we step out in authority, we are often the ones creating the wave.

About 70% of the time I might not feel anything when I step out, but I have discovered I cannot live by my feelings—I have to live by faith. I have to believe God when He says these signs will follow my life (Mark 16:17). He never said, "When you feel Me, that is when you know the signs will follow your life." He told us the signs would follow believers. That means wherever we go in faith, we can trust God's Holy Spirit will move through our lives and signs and wonders will follow us.

OBEDIENCE BRINGS JOY

It was 2008, and I paced my room in prayer one morning, asking God, "What do you want to do?" I felt urgency and knew I needed to do something. God said to drive 20 minutes from Redding to Anderson, and He gave me a specific location to go to. I had been to Anderson many times before. On Friday mornings, I would take a group of students there to minister with me. God had asked me to walk through the neighborhoods that were poverty stricken and rampant with drug and alcohol abuse. The police were often called into these neighborhoods. One of the men I took with me was Jason Chin (mentioned in the previous chapter). Jason had been consistently stepping out and hearing the voice of God, and he was excited to share the gospel with people. The transformation that took place in his life was amazing to me.

Jason came with me this particular day, and when we arrived we began walking around, knocking on apartment doors, and asking the people inside if they were in need of prayer. I knocked on one particular door, and I asked the gentleman who answered if he needed prayer for anything. I told him God has spoken to me and told me to come to this neighborhood earlier that morning. He reluctantly said, "No, thank you," but was excited that people actually came out to his neighborhood and believed God would do something powerful there.

Jason Chin was going to another apartment to talk to someone else and had walked by the door where I stood. As the gentleman I had spoken with began to close his door, he saw Jason. Shocked, he called out, "Oh my gosh! It's him!"

The man explained he had met Jason about a year ago. Jason was just beginning to overcome fear at that time, making a commitment to be activated in faith. Jason gathered a few people together, and they made a decision to do go on a treasure hunt. As they were sitting in their car at a stoplight, Jason noticed a bumper sticker that indicated a clue on their treasure map. Jason took a brave step and got out of the car while the light was red. He walked up to the car and introduced himself, saying, "We are on a treasure hunt, and we noticed your bumper sticker is on our treasure map. Is there anything you need prayer for?"

The driver of the vehicle began to cry, "Yes! Please pray for my granddaughter! She is in a coma at UC Davis."

Jason was eager to pray for this young woman, hoping she would come out of her coma. He not only prayed right there at the traffic light, but he asked for her name and hospital room number. The young lady was in the ICU at UC Davis (a hospital around two and a half hours away). Jason called the girl's father and received permission to go pray for her.

Over a year later, the man standing at that door with me was the father of the young woman who had been in the coma. This grateful father had desired to thank Jason for praying for his daughter. After Jason and a few others had prayed for her, she came out of the coma within a few days. The father explained this to Jason and me. Begging us, he said, "Please, please just wait here for a second. I want to call her and have her come over here. She lives right around the corner!"

We were shocked at what God was doing and how He was tying everything together so seamlessly. Jason simply went on a treasure hunt to step out in faith and love people. He had no idea what would unfold to him a year later because of his obedience. The Holy Spirit had given him the words to say and had led him the whole time! When I woke up that morning, I had no idea of the connection that was going to take place that day. I just knew I had to take a risk, just like Jason took a risk when he stepped out of his car at that stoplight.

We both experienced great joy as we heard this man's testimony and found out we would get to meet his daughter. John 15:10-11 says, "If you keep My commands, you will remain in My love, just as I have kept My Father's commands and remain in His love. I have told you this so that My joy may be in you and that your joy may be complete." Doing the will of the Lord brings joy to your soul.

THE PUZZLE PIECES CAME TOGETHER

In the spirit, we all labor as the body of Christ, working together to sow and reap for a great harvest. When we obey God's voice, we need to trust that He is doing things behind the scenes that we might not even find out about in this lifetime. When we get to heaven, we will see the impact of every act of obedience here on earth. We will fully learn how obeying God's voice, regardless of how small what He asks us to do may seem, carries the power to impact all of eternity.

Shortly after the father made the phone call to his daughter, she rolled up in a power wheelchair. Lisa was still in need of healing in her body. Her hair was missing, and she was unable to walk. The father explained to us they did not think their daughter would survive and come out of the coma, but miraculously, she proved them wrong and woke up. With deep emotion, this father said to his daughter, "Honey, I want to introduce you to the man who prayed for you when you were in your coma."

In great appreciation, Lisa turned to Jason and embraced him with an emotional reunion. That day, all of heaven came into this little living room and kissed a daughter of the King. We prayed for her to be healed completely and that the Lord would continue this healing. God had already done a miracle, but we prayed with expectancy that He would do more.

About a year later, the Lord spoke to me again to go back into this same neighborhood. We had already been sending teams there for almost a year, and I had even gone back a few times on my own. In fact, the Lord had once spoken to me when I was in this particular neighborhood. He said, "Chris, if you don't come out to these neighborhoods, false religions will. If you don't share the gospel, others will share a perverted gospel to deceive many."

As I went back there a year later, I took another group of guys with me who I had been discipling. I ran into a young man I previously knew from another ministry. He invited me into his apartment to pray for people. I did not even know what I was going to say, but in the moment, the Holy Spirit began to give me words of knowledge about the lives of some of the people present. The whole atmosphere began to change as the Spirit of God began to minister to people. Hearts were wide open for Jesus. As I was ministering, a young lady walked in the apartment to visit some of her friends who were inside. While I was talking, I noticed this young lady could not take her eyes off of me. She was looking at me intensely as if she knew me.

After I was done talking, she came up to me and asked, "Do you remember me?"

I responded honestly, "No... I don't think we have met before."

She said, "We have met. I was the one in the coma until Jason prayed for me. Remember when I was in the wheelchair, and you guys prayed for me?"

I was overcome with shock and amazement. God had answered our prayers! She was no longer in that wheelchair. Her hair had grown out, and she looked like a completely different person. A huge smile draped itself across her face as she thanked God for what He had done in her life. This young woman was a living miracle.

I share this story with you to testify of the power of God. You truly do not know what is going to take place when you step out in faith. The Lord is always faithful to show up. He will give you the words to say, and He will use you to demonstrate His power. As the Body of Christ, we get to partner with other believers in the harvest fields, trusting God will do something miraculous through our lives.

EXERCISE YOUR FAITH

When I look back on this story, I think about the radical journey of faith Jason went on and how he made a commitment to share Jesus even when he was afraid. When he chose to take a step of faith to get out of his car and see if there was anything the driver needed prayer for, it caused a chain reaction of blessings that followed the willingness to love others even when it felt uncomfortable. I honor Jason for that. To this day, Jason is leading his own evangelistic ministry and is impacting thousands of people all over the world, just like this young lady who woke up from a coma and walked out of a wheelchair.

God has given us a sound mind so we can track with the Spirit and be sensitive to hearing God's voice. He tells us to step out even when we do not understand the bigger picture, and we can choose to respond. Most of the time God is doing things behind the scenes. Our job is not to know the bigger picture but to obey as children of God. I look forward to hearing testimonies of what God is doing in your life as you step out and obey Him. Even if you think it is a small thing, you never know what God is going to do in the greater scheme of things.

When you do your part, it helps set others up to co-labor with the testimony of what God wants to do in the grand scheme of things. Keep it simple, have fun, and enjoy hearing God's voice. If you do not feel like you are hearing God's voice, revisit what the Word of God has already said. Trust in faith that God is leading and guiding you. He will never leave you or forsake you, and His Spirit lives within you and wants to transform the world around you. The Holy Spirit bears witness with your spirit that you are a child of God. As children of God, we have the ultimate privilege, through faith, to hold the hand that holds the world.

Sometimes it takes faith to believe God is with us, and He has not left us to go on vacation. Abraham was strengthened in faith by giving glory to God. Abraham was called to go to an unfamiliar land, and on his journey of faith, God met Him. God wants to meet us on our daily journey of faith. Faith is like a muscle. The more we use it, the more it will grow. Look for new opportunities today to exercise your faith.

I have found that the process of walking in love and the gifts of the Spirit are like learning to walk in the natural. I have never seen a newborn baby start off running from day one. There is always a process. They first must get strong enough to roll over, then crawl, then take baby steps, followed by running. You must give yourself grace to grow and learn as you go. I believe success should not be measured in perfection, but in your growth of learning to love others in power.

I have heard it put this way: "I would rather be a 'wet' water walker than a 'dry' boat dweller." Embrace the process of learning to grow in love. If you happen to get wet in the process, determine to never give up and to try again tomorrow. If you do, before you know it you will be releasing the kingdom of God in love and power everywhere you go. The world is waiting for us to give them a genuine God encounter!

Here is my "Love Says Go" site: lovesaysgo.com. Here is the Academy site: lsgacademy.org.

—Jason Chin

How can I practically apply this in my life?

___

What are the action steps I can take today to help incorporate this in my life?

___

CHAPTER SIX

EMPOWERED BY GRACE

"Faith is a kind of immune system filtering out fears that otherwise would paralyze all activity."
—Reinhard Bonnke

The grace of God is an empowering force. It does not just save us from our sins, but it equips us to manifest Jesus Christ on earth. In His blood is the revelation of God's love and His transforming grace. Grace is simply receiving something we do not deserve. It is the inheritance that keeps giving. Grace is never ending in our lives, continually empowering us to be like Jesus and to not entertain sin. This same grace that sets us free from sin and leads us to righteousness, empowers us to share about the transforming power of Jesus Christ.

Although I understood this revelation of grace, I continued to deal with fear. I remember the Lord speaking to me when I was around 20 years old to be a witness to others for what He had done in my life. Reading through Mark 16 and Matthew 28, I felt the call to go into the entire world and preach the gospel, but my desire to preach was overwhelmed by my fear. I needed the grace of God to help me step out of fear and into freedom.

As I was seeking the Lord one day, He spoke to me. "Chris," He said, "I want you to put on a Christian t-shirt."

I began to contend with God in agitation: "No! I don't want to do that! What if someone sees me wearing that shirt? What would they think of me? What would they say?"

I wrestled with my fear and God's will for quite a while, but quickly discovered when Jesus Christ is Lord of your life, you never win a wrestling match with His will. It is best to respond to His call and do exactly what He asks. In the process of obedience, He is preparing and equipping you.

In my wrestling, God continued to lay out His plan for me to wear a Christian t-shirt. I found a Christian bookstore in the area and made my purchase. As I put on that t-shirt, my face became flushed as I imagined people stopping me and asking me about my shirt. However, I knew this was exactly what God was calling me to do.

A little while later, I went into the local Wal-Mart, reluctantly wearing this t-shirt. The fearful feeling in the pit of my stomach cautiously reminded me that perhaps someone might stop me and ask about this shirt. Not even five minutes after I was in the store, an old high school friend spotted me from across the aisle.

"Hey Chris, how are you?" he asked. "Your shirt... are you a Christian? What's going on?"

With a touch of courage, I responded, "Yes, I am."

In that moment, I had a choice to make: to cower back or stand in truth. I chose the truth, which was that Jesus was in the process of changing my life. The more obedient I was to what He asked of me, the more He transformed me by His grace so I could be free from fear.

Eventually, it got to the point where I had to buy more Christian t-shirts because the one I had was worn out. The power of God's transforming grace was not in the t-shirt, but in the act of obedience. My goal is that regardless of what God asks of you, you would obey Him. In your obedience, the grace of God will flow to empower you to do what you could not do on your own. Joshua 1:9 says, "Have I not commanded you? Be strong and courageous. Do not be afraid; do not be discouraged, for the Lord your God will be with you wherever you go." He is with you wherever you go.

You may wonder what the big deal was with putting on a Christian t-shirt. For me, it was a huge landmark in my Christian walk. It not only required me to take a few steps, but it also required me to trust God. As a few months passed, I found sharing my faith became easier and easier.

Soon enough, my heart felt the transition. I approached the point where it became time to share my faith without a t-shirt. I must admit it sincerely scared me.

With reluctance, I made a decision to step out in faith, knowing God was working in my life for His good will and pleasure.

CHILDLIKE FAITH

The wonderful thing about the grace of God is it enables us to be childlike, learning to walk with God and holding His hand every step of the way. God is not looking for gold and silver vessels, but ordinary people like you and I that will say yes to Him and yes to the plans He has for us with a childlike heart. When I look through the Bible, I am amazed at who God picked to do great things. Most of the individuals were not super talented and certainly would not be picked by most people, but God saw their hearts even when they felt afraid—He saw they had what it took to say yes to Him.

As I continued on my journey with the Lord, I discovered that stepping out became more natural. The Lord began to develop a desire in me to approach people and ask them questions about Him. I wondered what it would be like if I took a camera on the streets and filmed while asking people questions about God.

It was one month after the Columbine shooting in Colorado when I went out on the street to pose my questions about God, asking, "Do you think the shooting would have taken place if Jesus was in the school?"

There were mixed responses. Some people were adamant it never would have taken place, while some were certain it still would have happened. That night, something shifted in me. It was as if my faith hit a new level. Although I did not know many scriptures at the time, I could feel the grace of God moving through me and empowering me in my approach to bring God up in normal conversation. In the process of learning how to step out, I was able to lean back into God's heart in full obedience, trusting He would lead me through this journey.

Much like a butterfly emerging from a cocoon, my spirit began to break free and fly. From that night on, I felt a grace to simply approach people and begin to talk to them about Jesus and His transforming Holy Spirit.

A short while later, I was reading in Mark and Acts the stories of how men of God lived their lives radically for Jesus. Although I faced fear daily, the grace of God was moving in my life to ignite and feed the passion inside of me. It was not a passion coming from my own striving, but rather from the heart of God being superimposed over my life in power and grace.

LOVING YOUR NEIGHBOR

I began to dream with God about my neighborhood being transformed. My heart felt a burden to know if my neighbors knew Jesus or not. I could sense the Lord wanted me to walk around my neighborhood and talk to my neighbors about Jesus. But what would I do? What would I say? These questions overwhelmed me.

All the possible scenarios played on repeat in my mind, ultimately feeding my fear and keeping me trapped in my cycle of what I thought I couldn't do. I kept hearing, "You can't do this," or "You can't talk to strangers about Jesus. They don't want to hear it." I feared people would yell at me or slam the door in my face.

These scenarios rolled around in my mind. However, one deciding factor trumped all my fear—God's outrageous love for these people. I too was a sinner at one time, saved by the grace of God. He wanted to communicate His love to my neighbors so they could experience the same grace, and He called me to be the vessel to be used to communicate that love.

I made a S.M.A.R.T. goal that was specific, measurable, obtainable, relevant to me, and had a timeline. I would walk down my street and around my neighborhood, knocking on every door, asking the people inside if they needed prayer for anything. Although I had no experience in this area, there was Someone living inside of me who had all the experience needed. His grace poured out over my life empowered me to do what I could not do on my own.

Approaching the first door, I shook inside. Each step jolted fear through every ounce of my being. Moving closer to that door, fear rushed through my body, attempting to control me and cause me to run away from this opportunity. It was in this moment that the comfort of the Holy Spirit told me everything was going to be all right. He spoke, "You can do this."

I rang the doorbell and waited in silent anticipation, wondering how the person on the other side might respond.

"Hello. My name is Chris. My parents live up the street. Today I am just walking around the neighborhood, and I wanted to see if you need prayer for anything," I said with shaky confidence.

To my surprise, I was not rejected. Not only was the man receptive, he even let me pray for him! It was wonderful to see God do something through me! I walked away from that neighbor filled with expectation and a newfound confidence. A new chapter in my life had begun to open up—a Christian adventure. I was created for this kind of adventure.

IN THE GAME

I always knew I was not meant to just sit in a church pew but rather to be part of a church that was active through the grace of God. I walked my neighborhood, talking to neighbor after neighbor after neighbor. Some did not want prayer, but I was not shaken or moved. I felt the pleasure of God moving through me as I continued to walk in obedience. I was stepping out with my trust placed in Him alone and not in my own strength. I found joy in obeying God. As people rejected my prayers, I reminded myself they were not rejecting me, and it was not a personal attack. It simply made me more aware of their need for Jesus.

My faith level began to increase as I walked through that neighborhood, growing in obedience and in trust. Faith was not birthed out of a church service, but by obeying the word of God to go and preach the gospel.

Jesus Christ was the ultimate expression of grace and truth on earth. It is by His grace that we are empowered to do what we cannot do with our own strength. His truth is there to direct and lead us throughout our life as we learn to walk hand-in-hand with our abundantly faithful Father.

SPIRITUAL GROWTH PLAN

Every day God gives us opportunities to grow when He asks something of us. When God asked me to put on a Christian t-shirt, He gave me an opportunity to grow in faith. This might sound like a small act of obedience to you, but it moved heaven and prepared me to respond to God's leading to walk door to door in my neighborhood. Every time you obey God, you move the heart of God. God loves it when we obey Him. Obedience, even in the small things, is worship unto Him.

A lot of people want to know where they can start, and I like to encourage people to keep it simple. Start by asking what is on God's heart and how you can help Him. Learn to be still and listen to His voice. One of the ways you know God is speaking to you is by the feeling of compassion to help others around you. Learn to have fun with God. Growing in relationship with Him is an adventure. I want to encourage you to take time this week to ask God what is on His heart for your neighbors. How can you help? What is on His heart for your school or work place, and what role does He see you helping in? Lastly, ask Him how He feels about the people you will meet throughout your day, and is there anything He wants you to do or say to them for Him.

For two years, I continued to share my faith on the street with strangers. The fruit of this was awesome, but I was not experiencing the power I knew was available. God has not only enabled us to share our faith, but He also sent the Holy Spirit that we may work in power and be a people who signs and wonders follow.

I discovered through teachings, testimonies, and literature that Jesus desired I would be baptized with fire by the Holy Spirit. Everywhere I went, I heard testimonies of individuals who had been baptized by the Holy Spirit and how it changed the course of their lives. Power was released through these individuals as they began to share the gospel. I knew this baptism of the Spirit was for me!

In the fall of the year 2000, I attended BSSM. During my time in school, God began to reveal more of my identity in Christ. I was nearly finished with school when I realized I was not satisfied with the life I was living. What God was doing inside of me was great, but I knew there was more! I heard stories of people stepping out in incredible boldness because they were infused with power, and the Spirit of God was moving through them to radically heal individuals.

Bethel Church's senior leader, Bill Johnson, would share many amazing testimonies about how God was moving through individuals around the world. My heart yearned to see the same things take place in my own life. Bill had gone to Wales for a brief period and came back speaking of the explosive display of God's power that had taken place on the trip. He shared stories of miracles, signs, and wonders.

Bill began sharing with our class about the Welsh revival, led by a young man named Evan Roberts in 1904. I had recently been studying the Welsh revival in school, and a flame was lit in my heart as I heard Bill share. I had a burning desire to see souls saved. I knew I needed that same Spirit to help me, just as He helped Evan Roberts. The same grace that enabled him to walk in obedience was being made available to me. The same grace had empowered me years before to step out and share my faith. This grace is found alone in the person of Jesus Christ. I longed that Jesus Christ would baptize me with His Holy Spirit and fire.

On this particular day, Bill wanted to pray for all the students in BSSM. He had us line up as he walked through and laid hands on each student. He prayed for the baptism of the Holy Spirit to fill us so we could be the living testimony of Jesus Christ with mighty signs and wonders following our lives.

Standing in that line, I knew my life would be forever changed. I told God in that moment, "I am not going to leave this place unless you change my life." As Bill prayed for me, I did not feel a single thing. I saw people around me being impacted by the Holy Spirit, but nothing was happening to me. At least, that is what I thought at the time. I knew God surely wanted to touch me as well. As I stood in line for another 20 minutes, I said to God, "I will not leave this place without being changed. I am so hungry for you."

Suddenly, I felt the lightning of God shoot through my body. It was like I stuck my hand into a live wire socket.

God's voltage was flowing through my body. I thought to myself, "It's really happening! He is baptizing me with His Holy Spirit and fire." Liquid love was filling my whole being, paired with a fire flowing through my veins. My hands violently shook under the power of God.

Then, God began showing me a vision of a young child standing next to me. I had no idea what was happening, but God began speaking to me saying, "Chris, will you go?"

I said, "Yes, God, I will go."

I saw different nations flash before my eyes. The first place I saw was Africa, and the people of Africa said to me, "We are waiting for you to come."

In that moment, the Lord spoke to me again: "Chris, will you go?"

"Yes, Lord, I will go."

While all of this was taking place, I could feel God's presence strongly upon my life. This was another infusion of grace. It was something I did not deserve and did not work for. It was a gift and one that could not be purchased. This grace given to me was to be stewarded, and I knew this gift was not just for me, but it was to be given away to others.

The Lord showed me location after location asking, "Will you go?"

"I will go," I responded each time, knowing with certainty that my commitment was more than just words. My heart was responding to His call.

I saw the people of those locations crying out, "We are waiting for you to come!"

This encounter lasted around 30 minutes before I began to feel the power and fire slowly lift off me. As the fire lifted, I felt something even greater being given to me. After class that day, I told another student we must go out into the community and look for people to pray for. I could not just go home as if it was an ordinary day. I had to give away what God had given to me! It was a step of faith.

The mall caught our attention, and my friend and I made our way over there. My friend had a vision of a young lady in a white tank top and knew we were to pray for her. Within five minutes of this vision, we saw a young lady wearing a white tank top, limping past us. She was with her mom and dad. As we stopped her, she told us about a sports accident that had badly injured her ankle. After explaining the vision my friend had, we laid hands on this young lady's ankle and commanded all the pain to leave. She looked up as tears ran down her face and said in shock, "All the pain is gone!" She looked at her mom and dad and began testing it out. She said to her parents, "I am not kidding. All the pain is gone!"

I thought, "Wow, God is real. His power is flowing through my life."

POWER ON DISPLAY

My friend and I walked a bit further in the mall before spotting a young man we could see God wanted to touch. I felt supernatural boldness wash over me, and I began to share the gospel with this man. The Lord prompted me to ask him directly if he wanted to surrender his life to Jesus. He confessed to being a backslidden Christian, desiring to give his life back to Christ. I prayed with this man as he re-dedicated his life to the Lord.

Something powerful changed in my life that day. In the past, I had shared Jesus and stepped out in obedience, but I never fully experienced the power of God coming out of me like He had in those moments. That day, my whole life shifted from fear to faith in God's Holy Spirit to move through me in power. It was through God's grace that I was able to minister with such boldness. Taking steps in the direction of God's grace is what empowers us to become effective in sharing the gospel and operating in true compassion.

"'Now, Lord, consider their threats, and enable Your servants to speak Your Word with great boldness. Stretch out Your hand to heal and perform signs and wonders through the name of Your holy Servant Jesus.' After they prayed, the place where they were meeting was shaken. And they were all filled with the Holy Spirit and spoke the Word of God boldly. All the believers were one in heart and mind. No one claimed that any of their possessions was their own, but they shared everything they had. With great power the apostles continued to testify to the resurrection of the Lord Jesus. And God's grace was so powerfully at work in them all" (Acts 4:29-33).

The apostles had already been baptized in the Holy Spirit, but they continued to pray for empowerment. They had seen God do incredible things in their lives, and they had even received their prayer languages. Over 3,000 people had been saved in their initial baptism of the Spirit, but they still were not satisfied. The apostles were radically aware there was more to God than what they were experiencing.

My heart's desire is that you become hungry for more of what God has for you. The apostles prayed a simple prayer: "God, give us more boldness." Instead of retreating and complaining about the persecution they received, the apostles moved in the opposite spirit and asked God to turn up the heat, crying out for more fire. As they prayed, the place was shaking, and they were filled with boldness. It was from this place that they went out and spoke the Word of God with boldness.

The grace of God that rested on my life after my baptism of the Spirit is the same grace that rested upon the apostles as they prayed and were filled. I would like to encourage you to live a life of expectancy for the baptism of the Holy Spirit and expect God's grace to fill your life. God's desire is to pour out His Spirit on all flesh. He desires to baptize you afresh—to empower you to be the witness you desire to be. As you read the scripture from Acts above, I encourage you to put your name in it and say, "Great grace is upon [your name]!"

How can I practically apply this in my life?

What are the action steps I can take today to help incorporate this in my life?

CHAPTER SEVEN

JESUS MANIFEST

"When I live out of discipline, I'm admired. When I live out of passion, I'm contagious."

—Bill Johnson

Jesus Christ manifests Himself in ways that are far beyond our understanding. He is the Great Communicator, Ultimate Counselor, and Highest Lover. His ways are perfect, and His heart is gentle and loving. When it comes to reaching the lost, Jesus has equipped us with the greatest tool of all: Himself. It is of the utmost importance to remember we simply cannot lead anyone to Jesus on our own. Only when He extends His hand will the lost who take hold of it be saved.

However, there are many different ways in which Jesus will use believers to reach the lost and reconcile them to the Father. No particular style expressed is greater than another, and God works in different styles through different personalities. All of the styles express a unique set of tools to equip individuals to walk out the calling

God has placed on their life and to effectively reach the lost in the process.

Proverbs 11:30 reads, "The fruit of the righteous is a tree of life, and the one who is wise saves lives." Wisdom is a requirement in sharing your faith and an attribute that must be walked out in partnership with the Holy Spirit. You may feel drawn to one style more than another, but it is important to remain steadfast, abiding in the Lord and listening to His voice in the midst of the process of learning how to step out in faith. Regardless of which tools you adopt into your own life to operate in the compassion of Christ, the Spirit of God will breathe into your life as you share the gospel. His breath equips us to effectively reach and love the lost into the Kingdom.

Friendship evangelism is one effective style in reaching lost individuals who you interact with on a daily basis. This can include coworkers, family members, or friends who are not yet born again. Friendship evangelism is birthed out of a heart-to-heart connection with an individual you love, encourage, and display honor toward.. Sometimes in evangelism, we want to see an instantaneous transformation take place, but that is not always how God works in people's lives.

When God spontaneously grips a heart and their whole life is changed right in front of you, it is both inspiring and encouraging. However, God also plants and waters seeds over time. This results in a harvest that is in His perfect timing and reaps a great reward. God works powerfully through this method of evangelism when we choose to intentionally love the unsaved people we interact with daily and put God's power on display through our daily living.

I recently heard another story from a friend of mine who owns a coffee shop. A few of his employees who were saved befriended an unsaved coworker. God's love began to move through these workers as their lives were put on display as living testimonies to the grace of God. As friendship grew over time between the believers and their unbelieving coworker, her heart was opened, and she received Jesus as her personal Lord and Savior. This young lady is now absolutely on fire for Jesus, and she spends hours a day in prayer, getting to know God.

How is this possible? People like you and me, who love the Lord, have simply made themselves available to befriend the lost and see God use friendship evangelism to reach their lives.

Friendship evangelism is not the only style God is moving through in this present age. Presentation evangelism is another method God is using to impact millions around the globe. This style is simply the ability to present the gospel truths in a systematic way. Evangelists such as Billy Graham and Reinhard Bonnke have used this method to reach millions around the world. They present the Biblical truths of who Jesus is, what He has done for them, and their desperate need for Him as their personal Lord and Savior.

Presentation evangelism draws a target where the Biblical truths represent each ring within the target. Suddenly, and without notice, we see Jesus is the bull's-eye by which our hearts must be gripped. Everything centers around Him, and apart from Him we are all lost. We are all sinners in need of a savior, but Jesus has already paid the ultimate price to bring us out of darkness and into His marvelous light.

The focus of the presentation is to intentionally lead those who are not saved into a relationship with Jesus Christ and for them to be born again. I absolutely love this method, because it presents the cross in such a powerful way. I have found this is an effective method to reach the lost while talking to unbelievers in both large crowds and one-on-one settings. However, this style of evangelism is primarily effective when it is motivated solely by God's love.

When presenting the gospel, the heart of the messenger needs to be so full of love and compassion that it overflows into every bit of the conversation. Sinners know they are sinning, and they need to know you are speaking out of love and compassion rather than hatred or condemnation. You do not want to come across like a Pharisee rather than a follower of Christ.

Reinhard Bonnke is a man well versed in presentation evangelism. He has seen over 50 million souls come into the Kingdom primarily during his crusades in Africa. However, God has recently been moving on Bonnke's heart to shift his focus to America and see the West covered in Jesus' blood—saved and transformed.

Bonnke's gospel campaigns have been effective in presenting the gospel in a crystal clear manner. After he presents the gospel, Bonnke gives an opportunity for people to be born again. Not only does Bonnke preach a message of Biblical truth followed by repentance, but he also demonstrates Jesus in power through healing both the physical body and the heart. He presents Jesus as the Savior, as the Baptizer, and as the Healer. It is wonderful to see God move in such a powerful way. I have news for you: God can move through your life in the same way!

The Holy Spirit is the greatest evangelist, and through His help, you too can present the gospel effectively to reach the lost and see many, many people enter into the Kingdom.

When I share the gospel with people one-on-one, I love to share the story of Nicodemus meeting Jesus at night. He asks Jesus of the miracles taking place. Jesus uses this opportunity to turn the conversation around and tell Nicodemus plainly that he must be born again to enter the Kingdom of God and to see miracles take place. Nicodemus is shocked, wondering what it could mean to be born again. Jesus lays out the truth to Nicodemus. We have all been born from our parents, but a spiritual birth must also take place. I love how Jesus outlines the importance to Nicodemus of being born from above, from a Heavenly Father, and of having an intimate relationship with Him, just as a boy would with his natural father. We see him then and there become a follower of Jesus Christ.

One question I often ask on the streets is, "Has anyone ever told you what it means to be born again?" Many people tell me they have never heard what it means to be born again, or they are not sure what it means. In these moments, I have an opportunity to share the gospel with them. While presenting the gospel, I am paying attention to what the Holy Spirit is saying and doing. It is wonderful to see the Holy Spirit touch individual's lives and see the revelation of their need for Jesus sink down into their hearts.

Street evangelism is something I really enjoy. It is where I oftentimes ask people if they know what it means to be born again or if they have a living relationship with Jesus. This type of evangelism keeps me on the edge of my seat. I especially enjoy activating and seeing those who have never shared their faith in their own community do this for the first time. There is nothing like seeing people experience the power of God at work through their life for the first time when they lay their hands on the sick and see them recover.

I remember taking a group of young guys out on the street years ago to pray for people out in our community. We stopped and prayed for a man and the power of God came over him to the point where he no longer could stand on his feet. His knees buckled, and he fell down to the ground, withering like a snake. It was a confrontation of light and darkness. The man's hand began to spasm and became claw-like. The young guys I had with me were on the edge of their seats. After we began to pray and cast demons out of him, we led him in a prayer of deliverance. He was baptized in the Holy Spirit, and he began to pray in tongues. This never gets old!

One thing I would recommend when doing planned street ministry is learning how you're going to actually disciple the people who get saved. This man had a powerful encounter but lacked discipleship. Months later I saw him, and he was in need of deliverance again. I know we cannot disciple every person we meet on the streets, but I do recommend there be some kind of plan set in place to help those who have an encounter with Christ actually grow in Him.

ADDITIONAL STYLES

A few other styles outlined in my book *A Practical Guide to Evangelism—Supernaturally* include:

- **Praying for the sick:** This method allows healing to open up an opportunity to share the gospel and how Jesus, as the Healer, is at work in an individual's body not just to heal physical pain, but emotional pain as well.
- **Supernatural Shopping:** It is important to create space in your every day life for God to move in power. While creating a shopping list, you can even add words of knowledge to the end of the list and see God lead you to these individuals while you are at the supermarket. Living a life sensitive to the Spirit's leading ought to translate into all we do.
- **Prophetic Arts:** Acting out a drama to tell a story of God's saving grace or giving a piece of artwork to an individual can be effective ways to creatively reach the lost. Although it may feel strange at first to give something you have drawn or painted to a stranger, it opens an opportunity to share an encounter with that individual and leave them with something so they do not forget what has just taken place in their life. There are many creative ways to use arts on the street. Allow the Lord to speak to you about how He wants to use your creativity to reach the lost in an effective way.
- **Tracts:** Handing out tracts on the street can be powerful if done as a way to share the Word of God, rather than to hide out of fear. When you value the written Word of God, you may want to hand it out in a way that others will have an opportunity to read it.

However, it is equally as important to communicate through spoken word to these individuals how much God loves them.

Keep in mind these styles are not meant to keep you in a box of what evangelism looks like, but rather to reveal how God can move through a yielded heart. God's Holy Spirit may be speaking to you to share the gospel in a completely different way than what I have shared. My suggestion to you is to do whatever the Holy Spirit puts on your heart to reach people, as long as it is done out of love. You cannot fail when your heart is full of love. Step out and see what God can do with your life. There is something incredible that God has placed inside of you as a unique individual in order to impact the world around you. It is time to step out and let the light of Christ shine through you!

How can I practically apply this in my life?

What are the action steps I can take today to help incorporate this in my life?

CHAPTER EIGHT

YOU HAVE WHAT IT TAKES

"God always works with workers and moves with movers, but He does not sit with sitters."
—Reinhard Bonnke

During my freshman year of high school, I tried out for the football team. I made the team that year simply because they accepted everyone. Each day I would show up at practice with anticipation, knowing practice always led to game day. But when game time came, I found myself on the bench. My position was nearly always left out, and I rarely had game time on the field.

The reason I share this story is because many people in the church feel the same way I felt. They go to church week in and week out, reading their Bibles, and their hearts are fully in it as they hunger inside for God to show up. They love God with all of their hearts, but they still do not feel like they are in the game. I want to encourage you that if you feel like this describes you, God says you have what it takes. Something inside of you is valuable far beyond measure, and it has the power to not only change a few people's lives, but many lives.

You may have gone to church your whole life but never felt like you had something to offer people outside of the church. I am here to tell you that you have something to offer that is indescribable—the King of Kings pouring out of every bit of your being each time you encounter a stranger with love. Just a simple hug can release hope to change the course of someone's life. Making yourself available to God and looking for people to love will alter the course of their lives for all of eternity as you step out in faith and partner with the Holy Spirit.

It is time to stand saying, "I too can become compassionate. I may never preach the gospel like my pastor preaches. I may never stand behind a physical pulpit, but God has given me a pulpit." Learning to recognize the pulpit God has given to you and the opportunities He places before you is one of the most valuable first steps you can take. This will help you begin living a life of walking hand-in-hand with the Father, as a witness of the resurrection of Jesus Christ. If you ever feel like you are falling back, just look up, get up, and keep going forward, knowing God has equipped you with boldness to preach His gospel.

Do not disqualify yourself if you are a new believer and feel as though you do not know the whole Bible yet or even many scriptures. Look at the people who God chose: He picked Peter, an uneducated fisherman. Matthew was a tax collector. God can use our past to set us up for success for our future. You cannot be disqualified by what you have done in the past if you believe Jesus truly died to cleanse you from all sins—past, present, and future. Dare to believe there is something valuable and amazing about your life.

Look into the mirror and deep into the heart of God. You will discover when you look into His heart, you look into your own and see all that He has in store for you. Make the decision today to discard every thought that says, "I can't." Stop partnering with every disempowering belief that tries to disqualify you and put you on the sidelines, or even whispers in your ear to just settle for less than God has for you. Take "I can't" and trade it in for "I can!" You can do all things though Christ Jesus who strengthens you (Philippians 4:13).

God is instilling His strength to empower the church for this wonderful end times harvest. Acts 4 is a great example of how God can take one ordinary man, fill him with the Holy Spirit, and use him boldly to proclaim the good news of Jesus Christ. The Pharisees and the Sadducees saw the boldness Peter moved in as he shared the gospel. They knew Peter, and they knew his past. So as Peter preached, they recognized something was different about this man. The spiritual transformation changed everything about him! The way he spoke was not in the way of an uneducated man, but as one anointed with the Spirit of God! There was nothing naturally attractive about Peter, but the Spirit was moving through his life in a supernatural way. God changed Peter through the empowerment of the Holy Spirit. Trust that the Holy Spirit will ignite you, empower you, and help you. He is radically committed to seeing you grow.

If you feel like Peter, where you have denied Jesus and run from the opportunities He has put before you, I want to encourage you that God redeems all things for the good of those who love Him. The Lord's hand is stretched out for you to grab a hold of so He can do a work inside of you that you never thought would take place. He will take you places you never thought you would go as you simply rest and trust in Him.

We live in a culture that loves to procrastinate. There is a subconscious belief that we are guaranteed a long life, but the truth is no one knows the day or the hour in which their life will end. No one knows exactly how long they have on earth.

In many Christian circles, there can be a tendency to look into the future and say, "This is when God is going to begin to move. This is when things are really going to begin to change. This is when families are going to be restored and neighborhoods transformed. This is when real revival is going to come." All of that can sound great, and there are even people that write books about it. The only problem is, it is not biblical. If we become so focused on the future that we forget about today, then we will miss the opportunities God lays before us each day.

"Your word is a lamp for my feet, a light on my path" (Psalm 119:105). God wants to empower us with dual focus. His Word is like a lamp for our feet, representing daily steps in the direction of our calling, while the light illuminates God's plans for our future. I believe God is preparing us with a grace for both the day-to-day abiding and to have vision for the future.

"Do you not have a saying, 'It's still four months until harvest'? I tell you, open your eyes and look at the fields! They are ripe for harvest" (John 4:35). John is encouraging us to have a double focus, and to live a life that makes sense in the light of eternity. God places opportunities before us each day in which we have a choice to lift up our eyes and see the ripe harvest field before us or to remain blind to what God is doing on earth. God is beckoning you to come forth and recognize how He wants to use you in the harvest field to be effective for the expansion of His Kingdom. You are empowered by the Spirit of Truth who will lead and guide you into the harvest field where the Lord of the harvest will walk side-by-side with you. Expect Him to show up in and through your life.

I hope this book has helped you, challenged you, and equipped you to peel away any disempowering beliefs so you will recognize the opportunities that lay before you. Compassion in your life will be fueled by passion for Jesus. I want you to ask the Lord what action steps you need to take in order to develop a lifestyle of compassion in action. For some of you, it may look like feeding the homeless. For others, it may look like fathering the fatherless or making time to mentor someone. It is so rewarding to serve the needy, hug the unloved, and mentor the forgotten. Let the Holy Spirit guide you toward the compassion of a loving Father.

Living life with a heart of compassion and developing a tender heart truly makes life worth living. Start where you are at today and make the commitment to say yes to what God has planned for you. Every day, God will give you opportunities. Take them as they come your way and respond to the leading of the Holy Spirit. Learn to listen and obey His voice daily. The world needs the God who lives in you—they need the God who demonstrates compassion with action.

How can I practically apply this in my life?

What are the action steps I can take today to help incorporate this in my life?

APPENDIX ONE

MY PRAYER FOR YOU

I declare over you new beginnings and new life in the Spirit. I bless you to live with childlike faith and to trust God with all your heart. I declare that God is with you and He has anointed you for such a time as this. I bless you to take risks and to enjoy the process. I declare God is going to activate the love of Christ that lives within you to impact the world around you. I declare your family will be blessed through the love of God that lives in you. I bless you to have favor with the rich and the poor, and to influence those in front of you with God's love and power. I bless you to never give yourself a hard time and to never live in the past, but to look into the future as you hold the hand that holds the world. I bless you to move and operate in compassion with action. I hope to one day hear about what God has done in and through your life. God bless!

APPENDIX TWO

SCRIPTURES ON COMPASSION

Philippians 2:1
Therefore if you have any encouragement from being united with Christ, if any comfort from His love, if any common sharing in the Spirit, if any tenderness and compassion…

---

2 Corinthians 1:3
Praise be to the God and Father of our Lord Jesus Christ, the Father of compassion and the God of all comfort…

---

1 Peters 3:8
Finally, all of you, be like-minded, be sympathetic, love one another, be compassionate and humble.

Psalms 51:1
Have mercy on me, O God, according to your unfailing

love; according to Your great compassion blot out my transgressions.

---

1 John 3:17
If any one of you has material possessions and sees a brother or sister in need but has no pity on them, how can the love of God be in you?

James 3:17
But the wisdom that comes from heaven is first of all pure; then peace-loving, considerate, submissive, full of mercy and good fruit, impartial and sincere.

Matthew 9:36
When He saw the crowds, He had compassion on them, because they were harassed and helpless, like sheep without a shepherd.

James 5:11
As you know, we count as blessed those who have persevered. You have heard of Job's perseverance and have seen what the Lord finally brought about. The Lord is full of compassion and mercy.

Isaiah 30:18
Yet the LORD longs to be gracious to you; therefore He will rise up to show you compassion. For the LORD is a God of justice. Blessed are all who wait for Him!

Daniel 1:9
Now God had caused the official to show favor and compassion to Daniel.

Luke 7:13
When the Lord saw her, His heart went out to her and He said, "Don't cry."

Zechariah 1:16
"Therefore, this is what the LORD says: 'I will return to Jerusalem with mercy, and there My house will be rebuilt. And the measuring line will be stretched out over Jerusalem,' declares the LORD Almighty."

Jude 1:22
Be merciful to those who doubt.

Malachi 3:17
"On the day when I act," says the LORD Almighty, "they will be My treasured possession. I will spare them, just as

a father has compassion and spares his son who serves him."

Matthew 18:27
The servant's master took pity on him, canceled the debt and let him go.

Luke 1:50
His mercy extends to those who fear Him, from generation to generation.

Zechariah 7:9
"This is what the LORD Almighty said: 'Administer true justice; show mercy and compassion to one another.'"

Nehemiah 9:19
"Because of Your great compassion You did not abandon them in the wilderness. By day the pillar of cloud did not cease to guide them on their path, nor the pillar of fire by night to shine on the way they were to take."

Deuteronomy 13:17
None of those condemned things shall be found in your hands, so that the LORD will turn from His fierce anger; He will show you mercy, have compassion on you, and

increase your numbers, as He promised on oath to your ancestors.

Jeremiah 12:15
But after I uproot them, I will again have compassion and will bring each of them back to their own inheritance and their own country.

Mark 8:2
"I have compassion for these people; they have already been with Me three days and have nothing to eat."

Philippians 2:27
Indeed he was ill, and almost died. But God had mercy on him, and not on him only but also on me, to spare me sorrow upon sorrow.

Hosea 11:8
"How can I give you up, Ephraim? How can I hand you over, Israel? How can I treat you like Admah? How can I make you like Zeboyim? My heart is changed within me; all My compassion is aroused."

2 Kings 13:23
But the LORD was gracious to them and had compassion

and showed concern for them because of His covenant with Abraham, Isaac and Jacob. To this day He has been unwilling to destroy them or banish them from His presence.

Zechariah 10:6
"I will strengthen the house of Judah and save the house of Joseph. I will restore them because I have compassion on them. They will be as though I had not rejected them, for I am the LORD their God and I will answer them."

Luke 15:20
So he got up and went to his father. "But while he was still a long way off, his father saw him and was filled with compassion for him; he ran to his son, threw his arms around him and kissed him."

Mark 6:34
When Jesus landed and saw a large crowd, He had compassion on them, because they were like sheep without a shepherd. So He began teaching them many things.

Exodus 33:19
And the LORD said, "I will cause all My goodness to pass in front of you, and I will proclaim My name, the

LORD, in your presence. I will have mercy on whom I will have mercy, and I will have compassion on whom I will have compassion."

Mark 1:41
Filled with compassion, Jesus reached out His hand and touched the man. "I am willing," He said. "Be clean!"

Isaiah 14:1
The LORD will have compassion on Jacob; once again He will choose Israel and will settle them in their own land. Foreigners will join them and unite with the house of Jacob.

Nehemiah 9:27-28
So You delivered them into the hands of their enemies, who oppressed them. But when they were oppressed they cried out to You. From heaven You heard them, and in Your great compassion You gave them deliverers, who rescued them from the hand of their enemies. But as soon as they were at rest, they again did what was evil in Your sight. Then You abandoned them to the hand of their enemies so that they ruled over them. And when they cried out to You again, You heard from heaven, and in Your compassion you delivered them time after time.

Mark 5:19
Jesus did not let him, but said, "Go home to your own people and tell them how much the Lord has done for you, and how He has had mercy on you."

Matthew 15:32
Jesus called his disciples to him and said, "I have compassion for these people; they have already been with Me three days and have nothing to eat. I do not want to send them away hungry, or they may collapse on the way."

Micah 7:19
You will again have compassion on us; You will tread our sins underfoot and hurl all our iniquities into the depths of the sea.

Luke 10:33
But a Samaritan, as he traveled, came where the man was; and when he saw him, he took pity on him.

ABOUT THE AUTHOR

Chris Overstreet is an evangelist with a powerful testimony on how his life has been transformed by the power of God. At 18 years old, Chris surrendered his life to Jesus Christ and has been transformed spirit, soul, and body. Chris has lost 195 pounds and credits his weight loss to God's grace working through his life to help him make better choices throughout the years. Chris is the Outreach Pastor for Bethel Church where he trains and equips the Bethel School of Supernatural Ministry students in supernatural evangelism in Redding, CA. Chris has a passion for souls and loves to equip the body of Christ to reach the lost. His passion for Jesus Christ is contagious, and it is common for miracles, salvations, and life transformations to take place as a result of Chris living his life naturally supernaturally. Chris travels nationally and internationally, preaching the good news of Jesus Christ and equipping the church to do the same. Chris is married to his beautiful wife Stefanie and has one daughter named Brielle Shalom. To request Chris for a speaking engagement at your church or ministry: http://bcrr.us/chrisministry

ADDITIONAL RESOURCE

The best way to describe Evangelism, in it's simplicity, is an outer flow of love and power to the world because of your committed, loving relationship that you have with Jesus.

A Practical Guide to Evangelism—Supernaturally has the potential to ignite the fire of God's love to touch a hurting and dying world. As believers, our first ministry is to the Lord Jesus Christ in our worship and devotion. Our second ministry is to be in community and fellowship with other Christians. Our third ministry we will never be able to do in Heaven and that is to share our faith with non-Christians. This ministry has urgency behind it because God's heart is for the lost, and His desire is that none perish but all have everlasting life. In this book, you will be trained and equipped to live a lifestyle of supernatural evangelism.

ADDITIONAL RESOURCE

The first of its kind, "Creating Momentum" presents four original songs combining passionate and uplifting declarations with inspiring, new electronic sounds. Chris Overstreet introduces the power of encouragement in an authentic and unique format.

Using both music and spoken word, he motivates you to set goals, follow through, and feel the pleasure and reward of creating momentum toward your desired future. Pulling from his own experience in overcoming obstacles, Chris serves as coach, motivator, and friend as he encourages you on your journey toward breakthrough in every area of your life.

"Creating Momentum" is a catalyst for change. It's time to start believing it's possible for you to tap into your greatest potential. You have what it takes to make powerful choices that will create momentum in your life today.

Made in the USA
San Bernardino, CA
02 February 2016